Churchgoers' Chuckles

Churchgoers' Chuckles

True Tales—You Can't Make This Stuff Up!

by Margaret G. Bigger

Cartoons by Loyd Dillon

ABB   A. Borough Books

ISBN   1-893597-02-4
Library of Congress Catalog Card Number 00-131766

Printed in the United States of America

ABB

A. Borough Books
P.O. Box 15391
Charlotte NC 28211

INTRODUCTION

Never will I understand why so many authors spend so much time trying to make things up, when true life is so much more interesting.

Since the early 1980s, I have been collecting true wedding tales—humorous, disastrous and outrageous. Many came from ministers, because, while I was seeking volunteers and funds for an inner-city church for 25 years, I would hear them. When two of these collections became popular, I branched out with motherhood stories, "senior humor," cat tales, funny lines about Charlotte and some true "male tales" and "givens" about men (all trade paperbacks).

Meanwhile churchgoers were telling me more funny stories that did not happen just at weddings, and parents were reminding me of the difficulties of passing along the faith. Ministers wanted me to relate their funeral funnies, too.

So...here are my favorites. But tales beget tales, and I'm sure you have some of your own. It's not too late, folks. There will be a Volume II.

So...if you'd like to offer your true anecdotes to my next collection, see the Contributor's Form, pages 95 and 96.

Contributors

Doug Aldrich *
Kathy Almond
Bet Ancrum
Bert Barrett
Trick Beamer
David Beverly *
Margaret Bigger
Randy Bigger
Peggy Blaine
Margaret Boyce
Susan Brackett
Carolyn Braddy
Martha Bullen
Maybelle Cagle
Jessica Calder
Marian Carlsson
John Charron, Jr.
Bonnie Chavda *
Von Clemans *
Lib Collier
Sally DePriest
Judy Dodd
Susan Durham
John Elliott, Jr.
Alan Elmore *
Allison Elrod

Paul Eshleman *
Leighton Ford *
Barbara Foltz
Bill Foster
David Friese
Judy Gaines
Marianne Grabania
Louise Hanks
Peggy Harrill
Holli Hart
Martha Hendren
Fred Hodge
Phil Hollister
Debbie Jones
Judith Justice *
Pam Kaczmarck
Jennifer Kelly
Mary Kerr
Tom Kinard
Carolyn Kirby
Cynthia Kratt
Thelma Kube
Peggy Lambert
Judi Leventhal
Carol Lockaby
Joe Lowe

Dega Lynden
Sheryl Manges
Greg Marshall
Frank Mayes *
Julie Menley
Camille Miller
Lucinda Miller
Nan Millette
Jo Minchew
Nola Mostyn
Kathleen Parrish
Nan Patrick
Juanita Plyler
Kelly Powell
John Quinn
Donna Reed *
Ruby Reynolds
Jennifer Rhyne
Jordan Rich
Janet Rose
Keith Shannon
Diane G. Shaw
Betty Shuford
Betty Simpson
Mitch Simpson *
Valerie Simpson

Howard Smith *
Ed Sossen
Loretta Spradlin
Marie Stubbs
Karen Stratman
Cindi Stratton
Karen Teitelbaum
Greg Thompson *
Jack Tingle
Jimmy Tomlin
Jim Wallis *
Maria Weed
Faeda Whigham
Dana White
Lynn Wilkinson
Wendy Willis
Linda Wilson
* Clergy

**Thanks also
to the radio
stations &
networks
named
on page
90!**

Not-So-Solemn Services

We all try to be respectful during worship services, but sometimes the unexpected happens. Quite often, that centers around an unpredictable child.

Having recently moved, the family had been church-shopping. Finally, they visited one they really liked.

As the collection plate passed in front of their 4-year-old Nena, she dropped in some Monopoly money.

Embarrassed, her mother quickly reached in and plucked it out.

In a shrill voice that only a child can muster, Nena shrieked, "*Don't* you take God's money!"

Mama dropped it like sizzling bacon.

"I got kidded for stealing from the church, but they accepted us anyway," says Juanita.

During the sermon at an Evangelical Free church in Illinois, Timmy came wandering down the aisle, looking in each row and whispering loudly, "Dad! Dad!"

Finally, the preacher stopped and said, "Timmy, your dad's right here in the front row."

Timmy ran up. "Dad!" he said fretfully, "I can't zip up!"

Mark was oblivious while his son, Trevor, 4, was crawling under pews and rolling on the floor of their Moravian church. Horrified, Melissa, in the choir, began pointing and making faces to get Mark to take control of their boy.

The only one who didn't notice was Mark. And the talk of the church became, "What's wrong with Melissa?"

Three-year-old Scott was misbehaving during the Presbyterian worship service. His father picked him up, threw him over his shoulder and strode up the aisle to the door.

The wide-eyed child implored the congregation: "Pray for me!"

Children aren't the only ones to cause a stir.

"We always sit on the third pew, right hand side," said Wendy. She told of the Sunday at her Baptist church when a doctor's wife came in late and settled behind Wendy and her parents. Glancing at the latecomer, first her dad and then her mom began snickering. Suddenly, the woman dropped to her knees.

Just the Sunday before, someone had gone into cardiac arrest during the worship service, so Wendy jumped up to assist the lady in distress. Then she saw what had happened. The poor woman's skirt had not been properly fastened. It had dropped off, and her slip was tucked into her pantyhose.

Meanwhile, a nurse had come running, and the preacher stopped the service to address the emergency.

Wendy quickly announced her assessment: "We don't

need an ambulance."

The minister mercifully resumed worship.

An Italian layman, giving the preliminary words before the offering at a Church of God said, "I'm quoting from the only book of the Bible that's Italian. The book of Mal-LA-chee says to pay your tithes."

Erskine told about his Uncle Johnny, a Southern Baptist, who came to visit his family in Louisville, Kentucky. Erskine and his wife took him to high church at their Episcopal cathedral. Uncle Johnny did fine during the Bible reading, but halfway through the sermon, he jumped up, "You tell 'em, Brother!" he said in a near-shout. "That's the way it is!"

Embarrassed, Erskine knew that his fellow-Episcopalians were used to sitting quietly in their pews and were surely squirming. But Erskine thought he knew what bothered them most: "He was really listening!"

A visiting preacher urged a Baptist congregation, "You need to stop trying to keep up with the Joneses by driving that Mer-cee-deez you can't afford."

Questionable looks appeared on the people's faces about the curious way he pronounced Mercedes.

Then he said, "You know...and when the payment is due, you're crying, 'mercy dees payments are killing me.'"

Special-occasion services: even more interesting!

During Advent, the minister was leading a children's service featuring an advent wreath. He had told them what each of the three blue candles represented, but asked, "Does anyone know what the pink one means?"

No one answered.

Finally, one little girl's hand went up. "Are they expecting a girl?"

During the "Words for Children" segment of a Sunday service in December, the United Methodist minister asked the youngsters gathered around him what they were hoping to get for Christmas. Several boys and girls called out their choices: "A Nintendo!" "Barbie!" "Legos!"

Then Stuart, 6, the son of a sports car buff, spoke up, "I want a Ferrari!"

Erskine's dog, Mimi, a 60-lb. royal standard snow-white poodle, was chosen to be a sheep for the Christmas pageant at their church outside Louisville, Kentucky.

"At all the rehearsals, Mimi was a wonderful sheep," said Erskine. "But on opening night, things were going real real well until one shepherd drops his staff, the dog goes 'woof,' and the whole thing falls apart."

That set Mimi off barking, the baby Jesus crying, and parts of the sets falling. End of pageant. Everybody went home. Mimi got fired.

At Christmastime, their Richmond, Virginia Catholic church called one of their services "Jesus' Birthday Party."

As the choir began singing "Happy Birthday," Ben, 5, began crying. He was sniffing and sucking as only a broken-hearted child can do.

"What's wrong?" his mother wanted to know.

"It's Jesus' birthday," he bawled, "and he's not even here!"

Just then, the priest stepped forward.

Ben smiled. "There he is."

Jean had to be at their Presbyterian church in Baltimore early on Easter Sunday, so she asked her husband Mike to dress their daughters and bring them in time for the children's parade. Libby, 5, and Kitty, 3, were both in the procession.

And so, during the service, Mom turned around to see her girls proudly parading down the aisle in their pretty new slips.

It's Easter Sunday at a United Methodist church with a preacher known for his long-windedness. At the stroke of noon, an alarm sounds: Brrriiinnngggg!

The "brrrriiinnnggging" continues while 7-year-old David reaches for the travel alarm in his pocket. Dad beats him to it. But Walt's hand is too big for that little pocket.

Finally, David wins out. But to turn it off, he must open it up. BRRRIIINNNGGG!

By then, the congregation is beyond reverence, practically rolling on the floor.

The South Carolina Methodist church was filled to capacity on Easter Sunday. While the children were gathered around for a children's sermon, the minister turned to a 7-year-old. "Ellen, that's a mighty pretty dress you have on."

In a voice that carried all the way to the back pews, she declared, "Yeah, but my mama says it's a bitch to iron."

Communion Comments and Commotions

It was the Episcopal rector's inaugural service, so the bishop and other visiting clergymen were present.

A member of the Vestry, John was helping the rector administer the chalice during communion. The church was full, and the wine was getting low. John turned to the acolyte and whispered, "Go tell Jason we need more wine."

The boy withdrew.

A few moments later, John turned around and there, on the altar, stood a gallon bottle of Gallo wine.

During a communion service in the Union Theological Seminary chapel in Richmond. Virginia, Von was listening attentively as a professor was pronouncing the words of institution above the bottle of wine and loaf of bread, "Make your Presence known..."

POW! That got the congregation's full attention. The cork had popped.

A visiting Episcopal priest, near retirement age, was red-faced and sweating when he was preparing for the communion. He kept wiping his brow and cheeks with a white handkerchief. That day, many parishioners, especially those on the back rows, declined to take communion. They wouldn't even walk to the front. The priest was wiping the chalice, the "common cup," with the same hanky.

Everyone loves baptisms!

A young preacher was conducting his first baptism-by-immersion in a small country church in Indiana. Two curtained-off rooms on either side of the baptismal tank, usually used as Sunday school rooms, were designated as dressing rooms—one for men; the other for ladies.

The first to be baptized was a small elderly man, followed by a very large woman. As she went under, she panicked and grabbed for the curtain, pulling it down. There stood the dripping wet, shivering, shriveled man, stark naked.

Terry, a Presbyterian minister, was holding Rebecca, 6 months, to baptize her. Apparently, he was talking too much, so she put a "shut up" hand on his mouth.

With difficulty, he continued and then handed her back to her dad.

The congregation was already snickering when Terry turned to ask, "Ever tried to talk with a finger up your nose?"

Barbara tells of a 4-year-old being baptized at a Baptist church in South Carolina. The child escaped from the preacher's hands—and swam across the baptistery.

Lee Anne was excited about her baby sister Beth being dressed up for a special ceremony at their Muncie, Indiana church.

She told everyone that Beth was being "advertised."

Revivals are a bit more relaxed, especially for teens.

Some of Marian's teenage friends liked to go to revival meetings in the Chicago area. They always tried to sit next to an empty seat so that when someone asked, "Is this seat saved?" they could say earnestly, "No, but we're praying for it."

A Tennessee woman told how she and her teenage friends used to sing, under their breaths, a refrain to the chorus of "In the Sweet Bye and Bye." It went like this: "In the sweet (wash my feet) bye and bye (gimme some pie), we shall meet on that beautiful shore (gimme some more)."

Not all distractions are noisy.

It's the teacher in her! Susan, a 5th grade school teacher, can be seen each week, sitting in her pew, red pen in hand, correcting the bulletin.

Why Ministers Trade
Wedding Tales for Fun

This is what ministers do behind the scenes, folks: try to top each other with wedding tales. I discovered this when I worked for an inner-city church and had to attend Presbytery meetings. That's how I got the idea to do *There's No Such Thing as a Perfect Wedding*. But when I went back to those guys to get their stories on paper, they would say, "No! No! The brides will find out we've been telling on them!" That's why all these wedding tales are anonymous. But they're all true—if you can believe ministers.

Being a mother of the bride is not easy until the ceremony itself. She may have had to take care of every detail beforehand, but at the ceremony, all she has to do is walk down that aisle, look pretty and sit in her seat.

A North Carolina bride's mother was nervous anyway. She stopped off in the ladies room of the Presbyterian church.

When her turn came, all eyes were upon her. And she did look lovely, her pink chiffon gown just a-flowin.'

But, in her hand, she was clutching a roll of pink toilet paper. Her pink clutch purse was on the back of the commode.

At the altar, the Boston groom was crying. Real eye-drooping nose-running tears. The video caught something glistening in the candlelight—a stream from his nose to his shoes.

A bridesmaid was furious with the maid of honor. But when her rival's hair caught fire from the candelabra, she suddenly had a great reason to hit her on the head with her bouquet.

She did so with a vengeance—and was a heroine for doing it.

They called it the "hot kiss." At a Presbyterian church in Spokane, Washington, a bride and groom had just kissed when a fire alarm blasted their reverie. The packed church emptied, as 350 people rushed to escape an electrically-sparked blaze.

Later, the couple signed their marriage license on the hood of a fire truck.

The only casualty was their wedding cake: smoke damage.

At a church in Mobile, Alabama, a groomsman appeared a bit unsteady. Like a green weed, he wavered during the vows. The congregation watched as he began weaving his way to a door, open it and step into a closet.

Immediately before the Virginia ceremony, the vocalist had eaten his fill at a picnic. So when he hit the highest note of the Lord's Prayer, it came out as the burp heard 'round the world.

The North Dakota bride didn't want to wear her glasses and had no contact lenses. Although she had planned to count her steps, she got confused and bumped into the priest. Backing up, she turned to the groom to start the vows. Silence. Oops, it was the best man!

A Charleston, West Virginia groom wanted their recessional to be the theme from The Lone Ranger, but the minister wouldn't let him yell "Hi Yo Silver!"

The groom was gazing out the window while the South Carolina minister was repeating for the third time, "Do you take...?"

The gazer was still preoccupied until the bride, twice his size, gave him an elbow. She knocked him all the way to the floor. "Say I do," she ordered.

He do'd.

There had been no rehearsal. But the Episcopal priest was nonetheless surprised when the jittery groom repeated a vow by solemnly saying, "I God, take you..."

During a Christmas wedding in The Citadel's chapel, a bridesmaid's bouquet (a candle nestled in a pot of flowers) began wavering. Some guests thought they smelled marshmallows roasting. It was the bodice of her flaming velvet gown!

A Baptist minister from the Myrtle Beach area told of a bride and groom who wanted their ceremony on the beach—in bathing suits—concluding with baptisms.

He said he dipped both of them in the ocean immediately after the vows. "I learned something that day," he admitted. "Don't do it when waves are coming."

The bride's one-piece suit had drooped to her knees. Embarrassed, she quickly turned from the crowd. "Guess who she turned to," chuckled the clergyman. "Me!"

All the while, her groom was laughing—until he stepped out of the surf. His suit had fallen, too.

The father of the groom was aghast. "I didn't know you could put tattoos *there!*"

A Missouri maid of honor felt faint. She sank to her knees. So did the entire Catholic congregation. "I didn't know I had so much power!" she said later.

Because the Greek Orthodox priest was out of town, another clergyman officiated.

The groom's family was United Methodist and "didn't know the drill." But they did wonder why they had never been instructed to be seated after the bride made her entrance.

Everyone, including the bride's family continued to stand for the entire hour's service. The substitute priest just forgot to lower his hands.

The priest pronounced the New Jersey couple man and wife. "You may now kiss Mrs. Metzer," he said with a smile.

The groom spun, stepped a pew away and planted one on his mother.

Oh, those pranks!

The best man was missing. The Baptist minister allowed them to hold up the wedding a few minutes waiting for him but soon resumed the ceremony routine.

When he asked for the ring, the errant best man popped up from the baptismal pool, snorkle and all.

Water dripped and his flippers flapped across the chancel floor, as he unzipped his wet suit and handed over the ring.

Only the musicians in the congregation caught on to the joke.

Pranksters had requested the tune "Funeral for Friends."

When the minister asked if anyone objected to the marriage, the groomsmen on the stage went into a football huddle. They popped up their heads and looked at the bride. Then they gave a "thumbs up."

In Albuquerque, New Mexico, ushers rated the nuptial kiss, as though judging Olympic gymnasts. The average was somewhere between 8.5 and 9.5. There were no 10s.

Never mind that the wedding was held in a fine Baptist church in Columbia, South Carolina. Captain Telegram appeared anyway, with his blue cape, his engineer's hat, balloons and diapers with a giant pin.

During the solemn vows, he strode down the aisle, grabbed the bride by the waist and began singing his telegram.

Now, wouldn't you think the father of that bride would have knocked him flat?

No indeed. He hired the guy.

Ushers, 12 of them, each handed the groom a ping pong ball as they met him in the chancel of the Greenville, South Carolina Presbyterian church. And what does one do with twelve ping pong balls? He deposits them on the communion table. The table is flat. Balls are round. Balls roll—ping—to the floor—pong. They bounce—pong, ping, pong, pong, pong...

By the 11th ball, the groom was handing them to the preacher. The 12th was a condom.

The preacher got it.

All the groomsmen in the Maryland wedding were military men who specialized in explosives.

When one of them was lighting a candle in the front of the church, it exploded like a firecracker.

Children at Weddings? Watch Out!

**My advice to brides: "If you want to have a
perfect wedding, forget the preschoolers; they're
unpredictable."**

The minister was expounding that "the world is up to its
nostrils in the muck of sin," when the D.C. videographer
panned to the 7-year-old flower girl picking her nose.

"I figured she was just doing her part," said her mother.

He kept making nose-wrinkling, forehead-crinkling
faces. Then the ring bearer started lifting one foot. More
crooked faces. More one-leg stands, like a stork.

Someone had put his shoes on the wrong feet.

She'd already peeked under the bride's gown. Then the flower girl, 3, wedged herself between the bride and groom. Meanwhile, the whole front row was holding up sticks of gum to bribe her to the pew. "C'mon down!" they whispered.

No way. She stretched herself out between the kneeling bench and the couple so the gum-holders couldn't see her.

The Boston ring bearer didn't want that ole pillow. Threw it into the congregation. They passed it back to him. He threw it again. They passed it back.

The cute little Missouri boy and girl walked in together. But the flower girl did not throw her petals. She couldn't. There were none in her basket.

Right after the wedding, Mama asked her what happened to the petals.

"Johnny ate them," she said matter-of-factly.

At Schroon Lake, New York, during a huge wedding with 16 groomsmen, the ring bearer howled and howled. But only while the groom's sister was singing.

The 4-year-old ring bearer in an Upstate New York wedding got hot. While the ceremony was underway, he turned and disappeared. Minutes later, he reappeared—totally undressed—stepped back into his place in the chancel, picked up the ring pillow and, as practiced, took it to the minister.

When the Kansas City pastor asked for the rings, the ring bearer, who was the bride's nephew, looked up at the wedding party with angst on his face. Then he began frantically searching the pockets of his jacket and trousers. At last, the boy pulled out the rings with a sigh of relief.

While the pastor continued, the little boy leaned across the groom's leg and gave a big grown-up wink of accomplishment to his father, a notorious practical joker.

This Missouri couple was asking for it: a flower girl, ring bearer and a miniature bride and groom.

The minister had said, "Let the children do whatever they want." That's why the toddler bridegroom was allowed to plunk the piano.

The only way the New London, Iowa family could get a tiny twosome to perform was to let them take pull toys. The ring bearer's wagon clickety-clack, clickety-clacked and the flower girl's duck quack-quack, quack-quacked all the way down the aisle.

Hand-in-hand the flower girl and ring bearer, both age 5, took such tiny steps with so many stops that the music had to be played repeatedly until the impatient 10-year-old junior groomsman pulled them to the front.

A fourth child was also in this wedding, not by invitation. The uninhibited 2-year-old daughter of the Scripture

reader ran 'round and 'round the altar until her mom lifted her up to the lectern. The little girl grabbed the readings out of her hand. Undaunted, the mother made up some Bible verses to fit the occasion.

As at many Catholic ceremonies, there was a time to "offer a sign of peace." People could give a handshake, hug or kiss as a peace gesture.

The flower girl had gotten into trouble at school two weeks before for kissing boys. But when she saw others doing it, she knew it was okay. She took off after the ring bearer.

The chase ended on the bride's train, where she laid him out flat and planted one on him.

Minutes before the wedding began, the 4-year-old ring bearer turned to his grandma. "I don't want to get married."

"Why not?"

"I'm too tired."

What Kids Learned in Sunday School

Anna's daughter Betsy was riding home from her Baptist Sunday school in Danville, Virginia with her aunt Sally.

"What was your Bible story about this morning?"

"Cowboys," replied the 3-year-old.

"Are you sure the subject was cowboys?"

"Yes," came the emphatic reply. "We learned all about a sheriff named Jesus and his posse."

Keith was waiting in line at a fast-food restaurant with his daughter, Kathleen, when an Elvis impersonator walked in.

"Looks like it's the king back from the dead," Keith commented to his 5-year-old.

A few days later, Kathleen's Sunday school teacher asked, "Can anyone tell me who rose from the dead?"

"Elvis!" cried Kathleen.

"My brothers and I grew up in a home with straight-laced parents in the worldly, sophisticated and wicked town of Clarksdale, Mississippi," reports Martha. "They were ever so careful to provide a wholesome environment with the right kind of companions and absolutely pure and sinless conversation. And we attended the Methodist church regularly."

That's why her mother was so shocked when Sam Jr.'s Sunday school teacher called the Monday after Mother's Day.

The teacher said that the class had been discussing mothers. At the end of the session, Sam Jr., about 11, raised his hand to say, "I know what Father's Day is."

The teacher had asked, "What day is Father's Day?"

He'd replied proudly, "Nine months before Labor Day."

In West Chester, Pennsylvania, Tina came home very excited about the upcoming Sunday school Christmas pageant. "We get to wear *costumes!*" she squealed happily. "I want to be a leopard!"

Her mother was confused. "But honey, aren't you

supposed to dress like someone in a Christmas carol?"

"Yes, Mommy." Then she sang in her sweetest little voice, "...was to certain poor leopards in fields as they lay..."

A new Anglican priest was teaching his first Sunday school class. He wanted the kids to think he was really cool, so he draped himself casually over his chair and asked, "What's gray and furry, climbs up and down trees and gathers nuts?"

No one responded at first.

But finally a boy said, "I know the answer is Jesus, but it sounds like a squirrel to me."

Susan and her husband were teaching first grade Sunday school at their affluent Baptist church in Charlotte, North Carolina. For several weeks they had been studying the prophets. Before moving on to Jeremiah, Susan asked the children if they could recall what a prophet was.

Their daughter Rachel was the only one to raise her

hand. Susan beamed. "My angel has listened and even remembered!" she thought happily.

Susan asked Rachel to tell the class, and the child stood proudly to announce, "A prophet is when you make more money than you spend."

The Christian Church minister in Madison Heights, Virginia was leading a class of 2-and-3-year-olds in Vacation Bible School. He was "dumbing down" the story of Jonah so the little ones would understand. "God told Jonah to go somewhere, and he didn't want to go," he said.

Brandon, age 3, raised his hand. "Mr. Tommy, Jonah was told to go to Ninevah."

Each 4-year-old seated in a circle in my Charlottesville, Virginia class was to tell how he or she shared. An obstinate little fellow stood on a chair, hands on hips. "Me don't share!"

True. He never did.

Parents and Grandparents Really DO Try to Pass Along the Faith

One evening, Judy told 5-year-old Kim to pick up her toys from the den floor and take them to her toy box on the back porch. Knowing that this involved a trip down a long, dark center hall, she added, "Don't be afraid. Jesus will go with you."

Kim thought a minute, then looked up with intent green eyes. "Well," she said, "if he's going, why can't *he* take 'em?"

The preacher seemed to be enjoying Sunday dinner at their Georgia home when Maggie's youngest daughter, Peggy, came in from the kitchen, carrying a cup.

She walked over to their minister and said politely, "Would you please spit in this cup?"

He looked at her with a frown. "Uh, why?"

"Well," Peggy replied, "Mama says you're full of holy spit, and I want to see how full of holes your spit really is."

Fred was sitting in their Assemblies of God church in Kingman, Arizona with his granddaughter, Natasha.

"Papa, I'm hungry," she said.

He just shook his head.

But Natasha was not to be denied. "But Jesus said if we come, he would feed all of us."

Fred got up and brought back a pack of crackers.

Faeda was at the beauty parlor with her mother. Suddenly, she headed straight for a lady in rollers sitting under the dryer.

"Don't you know you're going to Hell for smoking that cigarette?" asked little Faeda.

The lady stopped mid-light.

Humiliated, her mother apologized to the woman. She

knew, though, that Faeda was only repeating a message she had heard from her grandfather, an Independent Baptist preacher.

The woman later told Faeda's mom that she never smoked again after that. "I kept seeing Faeda's face telling me I was going to Hell."

In the car, Marlo, 3, was playing with a cell phone. Out of the blue, he asked Sheryl his mom, "What's God's phone number?"

"You don't need to phone," said Sheryl. "You can talk to him whenever you want."

With that news, Marlo shouted "HEY GOD! Can we come see you? Daddy can't come, but Mommy and I can come now!"

"Daddy can come later, " Mom mumbled.

The assistant pastor of their Newtown, Pennsylvania congregation asked Mindy how she liked church.

"Fine. I especially like the Halloween song and when you pass around the pizza crust."

Halloween song? Maria and the pastor wondered over that one until Mindy sang out, "Praise Father, Son and Holy Ghost."

But the pizza puzzle took a bit longer.

"You mean the communion?" her mother asked.

"No, no. When you pass around the pizza crust."

Then Maria thought of their after-church coffee time and commented that they didn't have pizza then.

"No, no. It's when you say, 'May the pizza crust be with you,' and everybody shakes hands."

Right before Easter break, Joe picked up his daughter, Sandy, from a Christian preschool in Owensboro, Kentucky. He asked what she had learned that day.

"We learned about Jesus and all those guys."

"What guys?" asked Joe.

"The Seven Dwarfs."

As Judi was giving Michael 5, his daily early morning cuddle, the Pennsylvania mom said, "You're an angel from heaven. God sent you to me."

Michael looked up at her quizzically. "In the mail?"

Janie, age 6, rushed into her Virginia home breathless. "Mama! Jesus is coming!"

"How do you know?"

"Daddy was out working on the car and called to him."

Marianne from Feasterville, Pennsylvania knew that Paul was having a test about guardian angels in his first-grade religion class in parochial school, so en route, she decided to quiz him to be sure he understood the material. "Who is it that watches over you and guards you all day?" she asked.

Paul thought a moment before he answered, "Nicholas!"

As in Saint? No. Nicholas is his best friend who knows karate.

At a Pizza Hut in Lancaster, South Carolina, Debbie turned to Julie, 5. "It's Preacher Karen. Let's go talk to her."

Their United Methodist minister introduced Debbie and Julie to her extended family.

Julie beamed. "I'm the church's alcoholic!" she bragged.

"Acolyte," Debbie corrected.

Thelma was helping her son, Kit, go over the catechism. "How many sins are there?" she asked.

"Two," he replied. "Mortal sins and convenience sins."

Some things we forget to explain.

While home-schooling her son Ben, Nola told him he could select a Bible passage. The 8-year-old turned to the "mark of the beast" story in Revelation. They then discussed the meaning.

Later, while in the grocery store near their Austin,

Texas home, they divided the list and went their separate ways.

Suddenly, Ben came rushing back. "Mom, it's here!"

"What?"

"You know—what we were talking about! Can we buy our groceries?"

Nola was still confused when he pulled her hand.

"Mom, you've got to see this!" He hurried her to another part of the store to show her two men with dark marks on their foreheads.

That's when Nola realized that she needed to tell Ben about Ash Wednesday.

Ed's son Eric was riding in the grocery cart when he yelled, "Look!"

Ed stopped the cart.

"Look—a witch!"

Ed looked where Eric was pointing. A nun was standing there.

Even adults get confused sometimes.

"Are you a Protestant?" her friend asked.
"No!" said Donna vehemently. "I'm a Christian!"
Raised a Catholic, Donna had become a Baptist after half a lifetime of not being affiliated with a church. She had always thought that Catholics believed in God and Protestants didn't.

How would you answer these?

A Reading, Pennsylvania mother, Julie had to chuckle when Brandon wondered aloud: "Can you imagine how big the naughty chair would be for God?"

Peggy was leading her family in prayer. Their prayer calendar instructed them to pray for the people of China.
Four-year-old Hunter opened his eyes with a curious look. "Why did we pray for plates?"

Martha from Walnut Creek, California was speechless when Claire, 5, asked: "Mommy, what kind of underwear does God wear?"

Another mom, Cindi from McCook, Nebraska reports the questions that stumped her: "What's Jesus's last name?" and "When you go to Heaven, does God have toilets?"

Benjamin, 4, had been rehearsing the Christmas play at his school in Houston, Texas. His mommy, Nan, had also read the nativity story to him and his younger twin brothers at home. So, before bedtime, he asked, "If baby Jesus was born in a manger, why were my babies born in a hospital?"

Katy was sitting on Grandmother Bert's lap scratching her leg. "Gramma, why did God make mosquitos?"

"I don't know Katy."

The 4-year-old thought a minute. "Well, when I go to Heaven, I'm going to tell Him to stop. We have enough."

On a Saturday evening, Maybelle was driving her sons to Mass at a Jackson, Mississippi Catholic church, when William, 6, suddenly asked, "How come Daddy doesn't go to church?"

Anthony, 10, took on an older-brother tone. "Daddy's a Democrat. Democrats don't go to church."

The 7th Commandment—not an easy concept.

Martha, now in her 70s, told about studying the Ten Commandments for her Sunday school in Clarksdale, Mississippi. She was practicing her memory work at the kitchen table while her mother was washing dishes. Martha got to the seventh and realized she didn't know what it meant. "What's adultery?" she asked her mom.

Mother's elbows stiffened in the sink. A quick thinker, she declared calmly, "Why Martha, that's when you stick out your tongue at your neighbor."

Martha clapped her hand over her mouth. Oh no! She

thought. I've done that with my *brothers!*

Every time she saw someone poke a tongue out, she shook her head, knowing that they were committing sin number seven.

"I was 20 years old," she exclaimed, "before I found out my mama lied to me!"

A member of a South Carolina Church of Christ told me about a little boy he knew who was reciting the Ten Commandments. His mother stopped him at the seventh. "Do you know what this commandment is?" she asked.

"Sure," he replied proudly. "Don't cut adult trees."

Mighty young minister!

"Mommy's being baptized!" Dawson was told, as the 18-month-old watched the service. A few days later, little Dawson performed a baptism, too: his teddy bear—in the toilet.

Children's Prayers

Repeatedly—four, five or six times—little Chris had come home from his Greenville, South Carolina school late and wet. His baby sitter, Joan, and Nan, his mother, had both punished him. Nan had talked with him each time, forbidding him to ever go to the neighborhood creek.

But Chris never admitted playing in the creek. He'd only say that he had *fallen* in.

After another wet-clothes episode, Nan increased the punishment. She confined him to his room through the dinner hour until bedtime.

Nan went in when he was ready for bed to hear him say his prayers.

"Dear God," said Chris. "Please don't let my feet fall off the stones."

Taylor knew her grandmother was hurting. She could hear her moaning and groaning. "I'm going to pray to Jesus to heal her," the 5-year-old told Dana, her mom.

Dana's heart was melting until her sweet Taylor added, "Because I'm sick and tired of listening to her whine."

At bedtime, Maybelle's 6-year-old William was saying his prayers aloud. He stopped to ask if it were okay for him to ask God to bless his class.

"That would be fine," Maybelle told him.

"I don't like everybody, so I'll just go by their numbers," he said. (Each child in his Clinton, Mississippi school is assigned a number at the beginning of the year.) "Bless number 1, bless number 4, bless number 7..."

Tom repeated a story his dad, a United Methodist minister, told him. It could be one of those "preachers' legends," but it's certainly plausible.

A father, listening to his son's prayers couldn't understand why the child began starting with "Dear Howard."

"Why do you call God Howard?" he asked.

"That's his name," said his son, who began repeating the Lord's Prayer: "Our Father, who art in Heaven, Howard be thy name."

The teacher of Vivian's Sunday school class in Chicago asked if anyone had a prayer request.

Vivian quickly spoke up: "Yes, please pray that my sister will get married soon so I can have her room."

P.K.s—Full of Surprises!

Greg, a Pentecostal Holiness minister in Rock Hill, South Carolina, was preaching when his daughter Ashton got away from his wife and ran up to the pulpit. In a voice which carried all the way to the last row, she said, "Daddy, Daddy, I go tee-tee all by myself!"

The library of a Baptist church in Chapel Hill, North Carolina featured live hamsters. Children loved to pay a visit to Abrahamster and Sarah.

One Sunday morning, the teacher of the preschool Sunday school class announced that she was going to bring in a special guest. She began to give clues to describe Abrahamster. "He's got hair all over, and he runs and runs and runs and then he goes to sleep."

Aaron's hand shot up. The preacher's son shouted, "My dad! My dad!"

His father, Mitch, has a beard.

Assemblies of God Pastor Lanny and his family were having dinner after church on Sunday. Nine-year-old Paul looked up from his plate. "Dad, who's Virge?"

"Virge, son?"

"You know," Paul said. "Virge and Mary had a baby."

Back in the '50s, a mother of 6-year-old twins was mortified when she found out what one of them said at their school in Rosemark, Tennessee.

He had hurried into his first grade classroom to announce, "We have a new sister, Elizabeth Ann! Now Mommy and Daddy are going to get married!"

Not true. They had been married for many years. Daddy was a preacher.

Evangelist Leighton Ford tells this one: A visiting evangelist at a small mountain Baptist church in North Carolina droned on and on. At 12:40 p.m. he was showing no signs of wrapping up the sermon.

Before her mother could react, the pastor's daughter, a preschooler, stood up on the pew, turned to the congregation and said, "Does anybody here know how to stop this guy?"

Michele's father, a Church of God minister in California, discouraged her from attending any parties where there was dancing.

She begged and begged to go to a particular high school party, and he finally relented. "You can go," he said, "as long as you don't dance."

He dropped her off, reminding her that he would pick her up at 10 p.m.

Her dad arrived a few minutes early, just in time to see Michele called up to the stage to receive an award for the best dancer.

Stewart, 9, was a P.K.'s K. Of course, his dad Jack had taught his children Christian values and clean language.

One day, Stewart went to a fishing pond in Travelers Rest, South Carolina, with one of Jack's business associates, who had "taken a liking" to the boy and bought him a fishing rod. As the associate was in the construction business, they were accompanied by some of the work crew carrying a cooler.

When Stewart came home, he went straight to his father. "Dad," he said with a concerned tone, "is it all right to cuss when you're having fun?"

Preachers Aren't Perfect Either, You Know.

Lew was preaching a very serious sermon at his Muncie, Indiana Presbyterian Church. He stopped abruptly and put his hand inside his robe above his heart.

The congregation took a collective breath.

"I've had this robe for 20 years," he said, "and I just discovered a pocket here."

When their firstborn, Andrew, was born Thanksgiving weekend, Betty and Mitch became the typical germ-paranoid parents. In fact, although Mitch was a Baptist minister, they did not take Andrew to church until January.

On his first visit, they raced into the parking lot with their precious bundle, stopped right in front of the nursery door and ran inside.

Thirty minutes later, during the sermon, a nursery worker looked out the window and asked, "Isn't that the pastor's car sitting in the middle of the parking lot with the engine running and two of the doors standing open?"

Preparing to perform his first worship service, an Anglican priest was worried that he would forget his part of the liturgy: "The Lord be with you..." to which the congregation would say, "And also with you."

His nervousness accelerated when he realized that the P.A. system was not working. He tapped the mike. "Something's wrong with this microphone," he said.

"And also with you," the congregation responded.

During the children's sermon at his Benton Heights, Michigan church, Tom, the young Presbyterian minister asked, "Any questions?"

A little boy raised his hand up high. After Tom's nod,

he said, "Yes, I heard you won playing cards last night."

The redness rose from Tom's white neck to his blond hair. True. He had joined a round-robin bridge group to get to know some of his members.

A Spartanburg, South Carolina pastor calling on newcomers was dismayed to discover it was the couple's moving day. The wife insisted that he stay and join her in the only room not receiving furniture: the large hall bathroom.

Was he embarrassed?

"Not in the least," Leonard declared. "She sat on the edge of the tub, and I sat on the toilet lid. We chatted for almost an hour. There was no awkwardness about it at all, until I rose to leave—and flushed."

On an August evening, Frank, a Presbyterian minister in his 60s, invited his two young associates for dinner at his home. One was rather tall; the other, overweight. About 9:30

p.m., they decided to go caroling next door at the home of their region's executive presbyter (fancy term for "head honcho").

The presbyter, who was already asleep, did not catch their late-summer slightly-out-of-tune Christmas spirit.

He devised a plan which he would carry out in December. On the neighborhood grocery store bulletin board and on the internet, he posted a notice: "A male trio (named "TWO" for Tall, Wide and Old) will come to your home, place of business or restaurant to sing Christmas carols of your choice. Call (their church's number)."

Who's had more practice at weddings?

Ever heard of a minister being the one to faint at a wedding? This one did. Thrice. The first time, he hit the floor solid. The second time, the best man broke his fall. The third time down, the best man and an usher stood behind and caught him. Maybe it was because this minister was also the groom.

It was a Catholic wedding, but a Presbyterian minister was allowed to assist two priests.

One of the priests instructed his Protestant counterpart from the side of his mouth: "Read the scripture." The Presbyterian obeyed each gentle command.

When the vows had been pronounced, "Congratulate the bride and groom" spurred him to step forward toward the couple. But he reacted too fast to "Kiss the bride."

He beat the groom to her lips.

In Fort Lauderdale, Florida, Pastor Mahesh was leading the bride Irmgaard and groom Peter through their wedding vows at his nondenominational church. The pastor's eyes fell on Bonnie, his own bride of several years. "Peter," he said, "Will you take Bonnie to be your lawfully wedded wife?"

The pastor prompted, "I Thomas...no, I mean, Peggy..." With on-stage projection, Thomas began, "I, Peggy..."

The groom was of a different faith than the bride. But the preacher had told him not to worry. "Just remember to repeat after me," the reverend had said.

And so he did.

"Dearly beloved," began the preacher.

"Dearly beloved..."

It wasn't his fault. The minister had been told the wrong time. So he wasn't there. Another preacher was on the premises, but he had never officiated at a wedding. The exchange of vows went something like this:

The clergyman sighed, "What do you want me to do?"

"Shouldn't you read from Ruth?" asked the bride.

"I don't have my glasses," said he.

Well, he muddled through the essential part somehow anyway. But when he got to the groom's "I dos," the groom added to the confusion with "Abba dabba do."

The minister concluded with, "Well, I guess you're man and wife."

But the bride was not sure. "Don't we have to sign some kind of paper?"

The visiting priest thought he was entering the door from the narthex to a passageway to the front of the church, where he and the groom must go. It was a restroom. And there was the mother of the bride on her way down to the commode, dress up, pants down, buttocks bare. Behind the clergyman stood the groom.

"I felt defrocked!" moaned the woman, hot with embarrassment years later. "And what came out was 'five cents a peek!'"

The bride was the minister's only daughter. Naturally, he was nervous. He had already made one mistake when he looked out toward the congregation and said, "I hope you'll understand if I become a little emotional. I never thought I'd be preaching at my daughter's funeral."

The rehearsal dinner the night before this New Bern, North Carolina wedding had featured "tainted" shrimp. Many people got sick.

During the ceremony, the preacher handed the Bible to his associate and raced to the bathroom to throw up—a *very* unpleasant sound over his wireless mike.

A golf ball dropped on the chancel floor, rolled and then clunk-clunked down the slate steps. It had fallen out of the Episcopal priest's pocket, a clue to why he was late.

The new preacher was thrilled to be confirming the marriage of his friends in California in front of guests from many states.

He said he wasn't nervous. But he opened the service with: "We are here to witness the consummation of the marriage of this couple."

When I was collecting true tales for my first wedding book, *There's No Such Thing as a Perfect Wedding*, two ministers from different states told me about what an acquaintance had inadvertently said at the end of the ceremony. It was the same story. I thought that was odd, but it was a good chuckler, so I used it. My publisher edited it out.

During one of my out-of-state book signings, a woman asked, "Have you heard the joke going around preachers' circles—the one about the minister who, instead of saying 'you are lawfully joined, said 'you are joyfully loined'?"

No wonder my publisher had left it out! I had assumed that, if a minister told it, the story must be true!

"My father's a preacher," explained the woman. "He thought it was really funny. But the next wedding he performed, it popped out of his mouth and he was so embarrassed."

Now it IS true! I re-instated it in my second volume, *You've GOT to Have a Sense of Humor to Have a Wedding*.

Inside and Outside the Walls of the Church

"I'm a pacifist. When I had my first son, I was determined that we'd have no guns in our house," said Allison, mother of two boys. "But I've decided that if they don't have them, boys would make them out of toast."

One Sunday morning, as they were headed from the car to their Episcopal church, she spied Benjamin, 2, with a toy gun. "How did you get that out of the car without my seeing you?" she asked.

Just then, they met the minister who was preaching that morning. "Oh, no," she thought.

But the minister pulled the Good Book from under his arm and made like it was an Uzi. Benjamin jumped behind a bush for the all-out shoot-out. Tyler, her 5-year-old, defended his brother with his finger.

Then along came a 90-year-old man. Allison froze with the thought, "Oh, wow, he'll be really upset."

With that, the seasoned citizen cocked his umbrella and "shaca, shaca," lasered them all dead.

Peggy, the mom of the only quads I know, remembers the church Halloween party when Curtis, Andrew, Rush and Mary Stevens, adorably dressed as four of the 101 Dalmatians, were frolicking atop the gym's bleachers. Suddenly a fire alarm was blaring. Parents and children turned to see four firehouse dogs standing below the alarm looking rather shocked.

That caused the large suburban Presbyterian church to change the style of fire alarms within children's reach.

Two years later, the same church, because of the same children, dropped the Christmas Eve tradition of passing the light candle-to-candle, person-to-person, pew-to-pew. Somehow in passing, Mary Stevens caught her pretty blond curls afire.

Oh, and which 2-year-old pulled the alarm? No one's talking. At 7, their motto's still "One for all and all for four."

As missionaries for Campus Crusade for Christ, Robin and Carolyn and their three young children, Mallory, Megan and Ben live in Budapest. While the rest of the kids in Mallory's class are taking beginning English, Carolyn goes to the school to work with her daughter.

One day, a little Hungarian girl asked Carolyn why she has to teach Mallory English, since she already speaks it.

Carolyn replied that she teaches Mallory how to read and spell. The child giggled and walked away.

"Mom!" Mallory laughed. "You just told her that you teach me how to read and steal!"

Linda recalls the "Christmas in July" theme at a Moravian family weekend retreat in the North Carolina mountains. While hiking and relaxing one day, they were to prepare to decorate a tree that evening.

"Imagine our surprise when we saw the tree with the 'nature ornaments,'" said Linda. "Four-year-old Leah had draped her favorite cotton panties among the branches."

A Baptist pastor was consoling an older member while her grandson Jackie kept grabbing her around the legs, yanking at her shorts. The elastic waistband stretched, causing the pants to fall.

Who was the most embarrassed? Not the kid.

While in seminary at Emory University years ago, Bo was serving as a Methodist supply minister at a church in McCormick County, South Carolina. On his first hospital visitation, Bo opened the conversation with "Hello, I'm your preacher," followed by "What's the matter with you?"

With that, the female patient lifted her hospital gown and went into great and gory detail.

"That was the last time I ever asked that question," admitted Bo.

In Zebulon, North Carolina, a Baptist preacher had stopped by the hospital to visit an elderly church member who was suffering from a urinary tract disorder.

"Preacher, he said, rubbing his abdomen with a troubled look on his face, "I think they're going to have to take out my uterus."

Red hair was not prominent in their families, so baby Michael's mom had a stock answer for strangers' questions.

One Sunday, as Mom, Dad, and their kids were leaving their Southern Baptist church, the redheaded minister patted Michael on the head. "Where did he get his red hair?"

Big sis blurted, "Oh, he got that from the mailman!"

Aware that Mass at the beach is usually a very casual affair, Lucinda finally gave in and let her son Jake and his friend go bare-footed.

Upon arriving, they found everybody else "decked out." It was First Holy Communion for two local boys. Nevertheless, they paraded in.

During the service, Lucinda thought "Oh no!" when she saw the Catholic priest glancing over at her barefoot son wearing soccer shorts and a t-shirt that said "Bud Light."

After Mass, as they tried to sneak out, the priest called to them. He led them over to a private corner, held up his robe to a t-shirt and said with a wink, "I'm a Coors man, myself."

En route to a New River tubing trip with their Moravian youth group, Bill and Linda stopped at a gas station to blow up the inner tubes, where Linda switched cars. At a fast food stop farther down the road, Linda got left behind.

About 45 minutes later, it was the pastor who returned. He gave her a hug. "I thought you might need some pastoral counseling about feeling abandoned."

As a child, Donna and her siblings were taken to an East Hartford, Connecticut Catholic church, but her parents rarely attended. As a divorced mother of three girls, Donna repeated the pattern until her friend Deborah invited them all to a friendly Baptist church in Hartford.

Deborah had told them to meet her there at noon. That suited Donna fine. She had time to do things around the house as usual on Sunday morning. She liked the church, too, especially their "dynamite" choir.

"I really enjoyed the gospel music," Donna recalls, "something our Catholic church didn't know about." She smiled. "The main thing I liked: they didn't ask for money. At the other church, children put in change, but adults were dropping in fives, tens and even twenties! I didn't believe I could afford to go to church!"

After several visits, Donna declared they wanted to join. At the orientation, Donna got a jolt. "I found out the worship service started at 10:45, immediately after the class." She had another revelation: "At the service, I realized that we not only were coming an hour and 15 minutes late but that they were passing the offering plate, too. We were just missing it!"

This dedicated Christian, who is now a minister, added, "I instantly saw how God takes care of babies and fools."

There's No Such Thing
As a Perfect Funeral

When I was collecting stories for *There's No Such Thing as a Perfect Wedding*, several ministers said, "When you're ready to do *There's No Such Thing as a Perfect Funeral*, come back."

"Oh no," I said, "I would never do that. People don't want to read about death."

But they told me funeral stories anyway. And I wrote some of them down.

Frank, a Presbyterian minister from Roanoke, Virginia, had to preach a funeral in Tazewell, about 100 miles away, on a cold winter day. While Frank was riding up front in the hearse, the driver said, "As soon as we get on the Interstate, you'll hear some interesting conversations."

Sure enough, a little later, a trucker on the CB warned, "Dead man on the right. Posies on top."

"Is that us?" Frank asked.

"That's us."

During the graveside service, sleet and rain pelted on the tent, collapsing the canvas atop the casket and bereaved. The mourners took off for their cars, and the minister soon was heading to Roanoke in the hearse. Frank told the driver how exhausted he was and asked if he could take a nap in back.

"Sure," was the reply.

He couldn't sleep, so for the rest of the ride back to Roanoke, there was no dead man and no posies, just a body that sat up every time they passed a car and waved at the stunned passengers.

A hearse was leading a funeral procession to the Florida graveyard when it veered off the road.

The rest of the line followed as the driver pulled into a service station to get gas.

Two elderly women sitting in a pew waiting for the funeral service to begin *thought* they were whispering. Both were hard of hearing, so everyone around them heard their conversation:

"How old was Ceil?" asked the one with blue hair.

"She *said* she was 84," said the multi-wrinkled one. "But she's really 87."

The blue hair nodded. "Ceil always was vain!"

As the organ played softly at Marian's father's funeral, she noticed that her mother was pretty well zonked out on tranquilizers. Then Marian heard her lean over and ask her other daughter loudly, "Are we having pizza for supper?"

When a nationally-known Baptist minister died in Lexington, Virginia, his obituary listed his wife first, "his beloved dog Daughter" second and his son third.

Phil's daughter Hope had read her father's "funeral file" and organized the service just as he had wished, with "Since by Man Came Death" and Handel's "Worthy Is the Lamb" for the music and a color scheme of piano-key black and ivory.

His former piano students, members of his current congregation and the Nazarene church where he belonged before he became a lay minister, many other friends and relatives—even his ex-wife—gathered in the sanctuary of the Moravian church in Charlotte, North Carolina for the funeral. Then Phil and his daughter walked in.

It was a 65th birthday surprise party, complete with a video of his life. He thought they were stopping by the church after supper so that he could put prayer cards in the hymnals.

At a standing-room-only funeral, ministers of two churches were sharing the pulpit. Marty's pastor was from a tradition that prided itself for having well-trained ministers. The other clergyman came from a denomination which does not require seminary training.

When it was the latter's turn, he told those assembled that it was time for everyone to "gird their lions."

Marty thought it was an unfortunate slip of the tongue.

The fellow then spoke of many of the deceased community leader's attributes, each time concluding with "We will miss him, but we must gird our lions and move on."

Marty was biting her lip and closing her eyes to keep from being irreverent. When she peeked, she saw people from her congregation doing the same.

Those from the other church sat stony-faced, nodding their heads. Apparently, they were accustomed to being encouraged to "gird their lions."

The twins' great-grandmother died. At the wake, Lissa, the most verbal, asked her mother, "Why is Gram so quiet?"

Sue explained that Gram wasn't really in the casket. "She's in Heaven."

Lissa scanned the funeral home. "This is Heaven?"

"The deceased hadn't done anything worthy," recalled Frank, a Presbyterian minister who was asked to do a simple graveside service by the dear departed's sister.

When he pulled up at the graveyard in Filbert, South Carolina, he was surprised to see many cars. Obviously, these people were honoring the saintly sister.

"We're moving the service to a small Methodist church near here," she told him.

So Frank rode with the undertaker to the church.

"It's a military service, you know," the undertaker said.

"I've never done a military service," Frank worried aloud.

"All you have to do is hand the folded flag to the widow," he told him. "But there are three widows and only one flag."

"So which one do I give it to?"

"The one who cries the most."

Frank watched the three women's emotions carefully, as he proceeded.

Just as he was to make the difficult decision, one of them

fainted. The result: chaos.

No one was handed the flag.

As a time-saver, the staff at a Lutheran church in Ohio set up templates for their worship folders on their computer. Whenever they had another funeral, they would bring up the funeral template and, with the search-and-replace function, substitute the new name in the appropriate places in the liturgy and prayer.

When Edna's funeral was being planned, they replaced "Edna" for the name of the previous woman.

Only when he invited the congregation to say the Apostle's Creed did the pastor notice that the worship folder read, "Born of the Virgin Edna."

Did you hear about the FUN-eral in Sioux City, Iowa? Clowns in full costume served as Delbert's pallbearers.

They were fellow-members of his Shrine clown unit.

When Mary Sue entered the funeral parlor to bid farewell to the deceased, she first greeted the mourners. A friendly person, she kissed many of women as they embraced. Upon finally reaching the casket, she discovered it held a stranger, like the ones she had just kissed.

Wedding guests were shocked when the chapel doors opened and, instead of ushers and bridesmaids, a casket came in. The music was appropriately somber.

Is this a joke? Who's in that casket? No one answered their questions until they had sat through the entire funeral.

The "rain plan" for the outdoor ceremony was for guests to go directly to the club reception while the wedding party held the ceremony in the chapel of an Episcopal church.

Some decided to surprise the bride at the chapel. Of course, no one knew to inform them that a vestryman had died and that his service had been scheduled for the same hour. The wedding followed the funeral.

Pentecostal Holiness pastor Greg helped his friend, who was dying of cancer, to plan his funeral.

The friend knew what he was going to say, but the mourners were surprised when Greg made this statement: "This is just the shell of a man. The nut is gone."

Family and friends of an elderly man filed into the church for his funeral. His wife was seated in the honored place at the front with her grandson at her side.

During a silent moment at this most solemn occasion, the little boy put his hands on his hips and squawked, "You see, Granny, I *told* you not to be so mean to him!"

THANKS to these radio stations & networks!

WASH-Washington DC
WMAL-Washington DC

Erskine Overnight
Janet Parshall's America

WBZ-Boston MA
WPTF-Raleigh NC

WRVA-Richmond VA
WRVX-Lynchburg VA

KIHT-St. Louis MO
KIXL-Austin TX
KKVV-Las Vegas NV

WVJS-Owensboro KY
WWMG-Charlotte NC

WGTR-Myrtle Beach SC
WJMX-Florence SC

WCCF-Punta Gorda FL
WMYI-Greenville SC

KLPW-Washington MO
KSWN-McCook NE

HYMNAL

Other Humor Titles by A. Borough Books
If you enjoyed this book, you're sure to like:

You've GOT to Have a Sense of Humor to Have a Wedding
Humorous, outrageous & disastrous true tales from the engagement
through the honeymoon + advice not found in wedding guides.
Margaret G. Bigger   Cartoons by Loyd Dillon   Paperback
Standard print - 1997, Third Printing April 1998   pp. 128 $9.95

MotherHoot - The Lighter Side of Motherhood
True anecdotes about moms from pregnancy through grandmotherhood
Margaret G. Bigger   Cartoons by Loyd Dillon   Paperback
Standard print - 1999, Second Printing June 1999   pp. 128 $9.95

MEN! Cry Flustered Frustrated Females Everywhere
True MALE TALES, GIVENS about guys, HOW COMES and
MASCULINE MISINTERPRETATIONS from 44 of those FFFs
proving that typical men don't think/act/talk like typical females.
Edited by Margaret G. Bigger   Cartoons by Loyd Dillon   Paperback
LARGE print - 2000   pp. 96 $7.50

Kitties & All That Litter
Mewsings, GRRRoaners, true cat tales and kitty limericks
by 26 cat-loving curmudgeons.
Edited/Curtailed by Margaret G. Bigger Cat-toons by Loyd Dillon   Paperback
LARGE PRINT-1999   pp. 96 $7.50

Gray-Haired Grins & Giggles

Guess What! Grammy & Grandy have a sense of humor, too!
True tales from childhood to retirement by 45 senior authors

Edited by Margaret G. Bigger	Cartoons by Loyd Dillon	Paperback
Standard print - 1995, Fourth Printing June 1996	pp. 128	$12.95
LARGE PRINT - 1998, somewhat abridged	pp. 140	$13.95

You Can Tell You're a Charlottean If...

288 ways that residents (natives, newcomers and long-timers) of Charlotte,
North Carolina are different from the rest of the world. Plus Head Scratchers
and a Queenz Quiz. 91 locals from all walks of life contributed lines.

Edited by Margaret Bigger & Betsy Webb Cartoons by Loyd Dillon		Paperback
LARGE PRINT - 1998	pp. 96	$7.95

See order form - next page.

What's Next?

You Can Tell You're In Charlotte If...
DaddyHoot - The Lighter Side of Fatherhood
Puppies & All That Waggin'
MotherHoot - The Lighter Side of Motherhood, Vol. II
Kitties & All That Litter, Vol. II.
MEN! WOMEN!
Churchgoers' Chuckles, Vol. II

Order Form

Please complete both sides of this form.

_____ copies of **Churchgoers' Chuckles**
        At the retail price of $7.50 $_____

_____copies of _____

At the retail price of _____ $_____

Plus $2 postage/handling up to 5 books; $4 up to 10
  books $_____

NC residents add 6.5% state tax on retail price to:
                                        TOTAL $_____

Autographed? Yes_____ No_____

Chuckles book to_____

Name of recipient's church_____

Wedding book to_____
Circle: Bride &/or groom Mother of the bride Minister/priest/rabbi

Date of wedding, if known_____

Motherhood book to:_____
Circle: Expectant mom   Mother   Grandmother

Names of children, if known _____

MEN book to_____Name of man_____

Cat book to:_____

Name of cat/cats_____

Senior humor book to:_____

Charlotte book to:_____

Your name/ address/ phone number:

Mail form & check to: **A. Borough Books, P.O. Box 15391 Charlotte, NC 28211**

Contributor's Form

Here are some true tales for **Churchgoers' Chuckles Vol. II**:

Please fill out name and address on the back.

Contributor's name_____

Address_____Phone_____

City_____State/Zip_____

Comments_____

_____

_____

Please mail this form to: **A. Borough Books**
P.O. Box 15391
Charlotte, NC 28211